DATE DUE

11/6	

$14.30

THE YOUNG AUTHOR'S DO-IT-YOURSELF BOOK

HOW TO WRITE, ILLUSTRATE, AND PRODUCE YOUR OWN BOOK

Donna Guthrie, Nancy Bentley, and Katy Keck Arnsteen

Illustrated by Katy Keck Arnsteen

The Millbrook Press · Brookfield, Connecticut

THIS BOOK IS DEDICATED TO ALL YOUNG PEOPLE WHO WANT TO SEE THEIR STORIES TURNED INTO BOOKS.

Published by The Millbrook Press
2 Old New Milford Road, Brookfield, Connecticut 06804

Library of Congress Cataloging-in-Publication Data
Guthrie, Donna.
The young author's do-it-yourself book : how to write, illustrate,
and produce your own book / by Donna Guthrie, Nancy Bentley,
and Katy Keck Arnsteen ; illustrated by Katy Keck Arnsteen.
p.   cm.
Includes index.
Summary: Provides step-by-step instructions on how to write a
fiction or nonfiction story, illustrate it, and assemble it as a
hand-bound book.
ISBN 1-56294-350-2 (lib. bdg.) ISBN 1-56294-723-0 (pbk.)
1. Books—Juvenile literature.   2. Authorship—Juvenile
literature.   3. Book industries and trade—Juvenile literature.
[1. Books.   2. Authorship.]   I. Bentley, Nancy.   II. Arnsteen,
Katy Keck.   III. Title.
Z116.A2G87   1994
070.5′93—dc20   93-9736 CIP AC

CONTENTS

INTRODUCTION

Books, books, books! For as long as you can remember you have been surrounded by books. Story books, encyclopedias, dictionaries, phone books, and many, many others.

Some books carry us to faraway worlds. Some books send chills down our spines. Some books tug at our hearts and make us cry, while others spark our imagination and tickle our funny bone.

Some books give us facts. Some tell us about the world we live in.

Some books we can carry in our back pockets. Some books are so big we can't even pick them up.

Books have been written so that important stories and ideas can be read over and over again. Do *you* have a story you would like people to read? Would you like to make your story into a book?

If so, then this is the book for you!

This book is a step-by-step guide on how to write your own story, draw your own pictures, and produce your own book.

STEP ONE

STEP TWO

STEP THREE

STEP FOUR

STEP FIVE

WRITING

How to start?

Put on your author's hat!
It's the author's job to write
the story.

A story can be fiction or
nonfiction. What would you
like to write?

WHAT IS FICTION?

Fiction is something that you make up from your own imagination.

Everyone has a story inside, waiting to be told.

Your job is to write that story.

Famous writers will tell you to "write about the things you know!" Think about something that has happened to you. Can you write a story about it? Often authors take a memory and build a story around it. You can do that, too.

I KNOW ABOUT 🐱s, 🦇s, AND 🐝s AND 🐟 THAT SWIM UPSTREAM.

I KNOW ABOUT ✈s, 🚂s, AND ⚾s AND THINGS NOT AS THEY SEEM.

To get your memory maker started, here are some story suggestions for you.

Have you ever thought about an enchanted place and magical things? Imagine a kingdom of your very own. *Write about it.*

Were you ever scared of someone or something? Imagine a mystery story using that person or place. *Write about it.*

Did you ever read about outer space? Imagine that you discover a new planet. *Write about it.*

Did you ever fly on a plane, ride on a train, or paddle your own canoe? Imagine a trip around the world. *Write about it.*

Have you ever been lost? What were your feelings? Imagine yourself lost in the woods. *Write about it.*

Sometimes authors want to make their stories more exciting. They ask the magic question *"what if?"*

This question turns everyday things upside down. It helps authors see ordinary things in an unusual way.

1 WHAT IF YOUR DOG COULD TALK? WHAT WOULD HE SAY?

GIMME A PET!

2 WHAT IF YOUR AUNT ANNIE LIVED IN THE NORTH POLE AND HER BEST FRIEND WAS A POLAR BEAR WHO LIKED HOT WEATHER?

3 WHAT IF YOU HAD A FLYING CARPET? WHERE WOULD YOU GO?

4 WHAT IF KILLER BEES ATTACKED YOUR NEIGHBORHOOD?

5 WHAT IF YOU WOKE UP ONE MORNING AND FOUND YOURSELF AS SMALL AS A MOUSE?

6 WHAT IF YOU LIVED IN A WORLD WHERE ANIMALS WERE IN CHARGE AND PEOPLE WERE THEIR PETS?

7 WHAT IF YOU CREATED A GAME WHERE EVERYBODY WINS?

8 WHAT IF THERE WERE NO SCHOOLS? WHAT WOULD YOUR LIFE BE LIKE?

9 WHAT IF YOU WERE BORN OLD AND GREW YOUNGER?

10 WHAT IF YOU COULD BREATHE UNDER WATER? HOW WOULD THAT CHANGE YOUR LIFE?

WRITE ABOUT IT.

There are many roads to a good story. The choice is up to you.

Have you decided which way to go? Then pack your backpack. You'll need these things:

Characters	A Problem
A Setting	A Solution

If the story is interesting to you, it will be interesting to others.

If it is a funny story, try to make your reader laugh out loud.

If it is a scary story, try to make your reader shiver with suspense.

If your story is sad, try to make your reader feel it deep within his or her heart.

Be sure to write your story in the most exciting way you can.

CHARACTERS

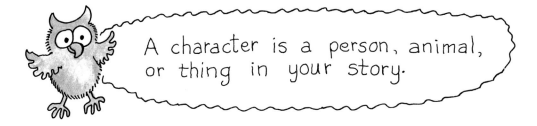

A character is a person, animal, or thing in your story.

All good stories have interesting characters.

In a good story the main character has a problem. When you write your story you will show how the main character solves the problem.

Choose your characters carefully. You will be writing all about them and their adventures. It is important that you like them.

SETTINGS

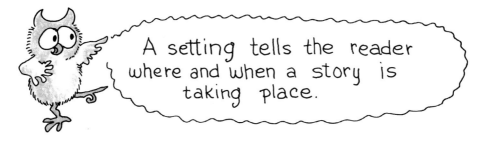

A setting tells the reader where and when a story is taking place.

A setting could be in Africa, in outer space, or in the magical kingdom of Oz. The reader must know *when* the story takes place. Did the story happen yesterday? Today? Or tomorrow?

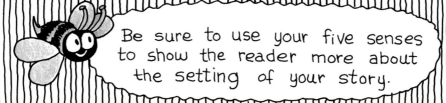

Be sure to use your five senses to show the reader more about the setting of your story.

If your story is set in Africa . . .

 Make your reader hear
the roar of a lion
and the beat of an African drum.

Make your reader spy the leopard spots
and see the jaguar run.

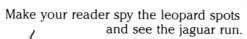 Make your reader smell
the campfire smoke
and the grass so deep and dry.

Make your reader taste the fresh sweet mango
as the animals go walking by.

 Make your reader feel
the warmth of Africa,
the heat of the desert sun.

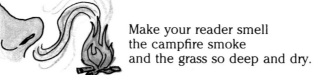

When your reader senses Africa, then you know your work is done!

PROBLEM

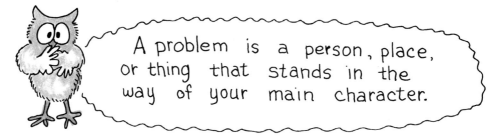

A problem is a person, place, or thing that stands in the way of your main character.

If your character has no problem to solve, there is no story to write about.

If Little Red Riding Hood hadn't met the wolf, she would have gone straight to her grandmother's house. No problem.

But . . . she wandered off the path and met the Big Bad Wolf. Big problem!

See how many problems you can throw in the path of your character. What if the Big Bad Wolf was frightened to death of little girls in red capes?

SOLUTION

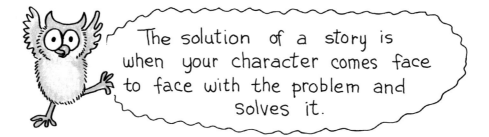

The solution of a story is when your character comes face to face with the problem and solves it.

Throughout the story, you should give your main character ideas or tools that will help him or her solve the problem.

For instance, if your character has to escape from an angry bear, make sure he can run fast!

Make sure that your readers know about your character's abilities, too! If your main character must read an ancient Egyptian map, make sure she can read hieroglyphics.

Be sure that a thread of truth or logic runs throughout your story. If your main character is a little boy who has shrunk to the size of a gerbil, don't have him put an orange in his pocket.

As you travel the road to a good story, you will notice that it has a beginning, a middle, and an end.

In the beginning of your story, we meet the main character and find out what the problem is.

In the middle of the story, your character has a number of adventures trying to solve the problem.

At the end of your story, your character has solved the problem and has changed in some way.

Be sure to tie up all loose ends in your story. Don't leave any characters or problems dangling!

Reading a bad story is like plodding across a flat sandy desert. There are no hills, no bumps, nothing to look forward to. A bad story moves slowly, has no surprises, and lacks excitement. It's boring.

Reading a good story is like taking a hike through the mountains. You never know what's around the bend or over the next hill.

A good story has twists, turns, and surprises. You can't wait to find out what happens next. It's exciting!

THE MOUNTAIN CLIMBER'S METHOD OF
PLANNING AND WRITING A GOOD STORY

Think about these questions. When you can answer them all you're ready to set off and write your story.

Beginning: When and where does the story take place?
Who are the characters?
What is the main character's problem?

Middle: What does the main character do to solve the problem?
What adventures happen along the way?

Climax: Does your character solve the problem? This should be the most exciting part of your story.

End: Are all the loose ends tied up?
Does the main character change in some way?

BEGINNING   MIDDLE   END

TEN RULES FOR A GOOD STORY

1. Make your main character both interesting and likable.
2. Show your character's problem right away.
3. Have your character say things that move the story.
4. Don't put too many characters in your story.
5. Keep your story simple.
6. Keep the story moving with lots of action.
7. Keep your story exciting . . . use action words.
8. Choose one style and stick with it.
   If your story starts out funny, it should have a funny ending.
9. Try to avoid ending your story this way: "It was all just a dream."
10. End your story on a positive note.

WHAT IS NONFICTION?

Nonfiction is factual and based on research.

Where do facts come from?
    Facts are found in many places. Your library
    is filled with different types of information.

When you are in the library check into:
    Encyclopedias, magazines, newspapers, taped
    interviews, computer data bases, photographs,
    maps, films, and videos.

There are many different types of nonfiction stories.

Some nonfiction stories tell you how to do something. These are *how-to* stories.

Some nonfiction stories are about your life and the things that have happened to you. These are *personal experience* stories.

Some nonfiction stories are about other people and their lives. These are *interviews* and *biographies*.

Or a nonfiction story could be about something you've read and found interesting. These are *factual reports*.

In all these kinds of stories, the facts must be true.

AN INTERVIEW

An interview story is about a person who has accomplished something or lived an interesting life.

At the beginning of your story describe the person and tell the reader why this person is interesting.

There are two ways to write about the interview.

One is the question (Q) and answer (A) way:

(Q) Do you have any sisters or brothers?

(A) I have three younger sisters and an older brother.

Another way is to summarize what the person said and use quotes.

Mr. Jones comes from a big family. "I have three younger sisters and an older brother," he said.

At the end, remind readers why this person is special.

A HOW-TO BOOK

A how-to book tells how to make something or do something.

All good how-to stories are about subjects that will interest your reader. In a how-to story:

1. Tell the reader what the project will be.
2. Tell the reader what materials are needed and how much time it will take to do it. Be specific.
3. Give simple step-by-step instructions.
4. Alert the reader about what could go wrong.
5. Tell how the completed project should look. If you can draw a picture or take a photograph of the completed project, that will help the reader.
6. Be sure to tell readers how much fun the project is, so that they will want to do it.

A PERSONAL EXPERIENCE

A good personal experience story tells something exciting or unusual that has happened to you.

Choose an event that changed you in some way. It can be funny, inspiring, or exciting.

Tell the story the way it happened.
Try to make the reader *feel* what happened to you.
Make sure the reader understands what you learned from this experience.

THE BEST PRESENT I EVER GOT by Bo Ribbon

WHEN MY SNOWMAN MELTED BY I. C. COLE

The Day My Brother Was Born BY KAREN BURP

I SWALLOWED A NICKEL BY Moni Mint

A FACTUAL REPORT

A factual story informs the reader about a topic using information from other sources.

A factual story can:

Give the reader new facts about a subject.
Change the reader's point of view.
Persuade the reader to do or not to do something.
Explain a complicated idea in a simple way.
Look at forgotten facts or ideas.

Newspaper Joe,
Newspaper Joe,
Was a newspaper man
From his head to his toe.

One day on his beat,
One day on his beat,
Who robbed the bank?
It was bank robber Pete.

Pete ran past Joe.
Pete ran past Joe.
What did Pete carry?
A bag full of dough.

Joe looked at the time.
Joe looked at the time.
When did it happen?
It was half past nine.

It started to rain.
It started to rain.
Where did this happen?
It happened on Main.

It started to pour.
It started to pour.
Why did Pete stop?
His wet paper bag tore.

Pete dropped the money.
Pete dropped the money.
How did it end?
The story's quite funny.

Pete fell on the ground.
Pete fell on the ground.
Joe wrote the story
As police gathered round.

The idea for a nonfiction story can come from anywhere. For instance, one day you're making a peanut butter and jelly sandwich. As you spread the jelly you begin to wonder about the bread.

When and where was the first bread made?
This would be a good history report.

What goes into bread? What makes bread rise?
This would make a good science report.

Who makes pizza in your town?
You could interview the owner of the local pizzeria.

Does your grandmother have a favorite bread recipe?
This would make the beginning of a how-to story.

When and where was the largest loaf of bread baked?
These facts would make a good newspaper story.

Sometimes authors are curious about the things around them. Truth is often stranger than fiction. They ask themselves the magic question "*what about?*" This turns everyday things into exciting questions. It helps authors to wonder how things work. What's inside? What makes it tick?

1 DO YOU HAVE A SPECIAL HOBBY?

2 DO YOU COLLECT THINGS?

3 DO YOU LIKE A SPECIAL SPORT?

4 DO YOU HAVE A FAVORITE WILD ANIMAL?

5 DO YOU ADMIRE SOMEONE SPECIAL?

6 DO YOU WRITE POETRY, SONGS, OR RHYMES? COLLECT THEM AND MAKE A BOOK.

7 DO YOU WANT TO KNOW MORE ABOUT OUTER SPACE?

8 DO YOU LIKE PUZZLES OR SECRET CODES? PUT THEM TOGETHER IN A BOOK.

9 DO YOU LIKE BUGS AND CREEPY CRAWLY THINGS?

10 CAN YOU MAKE SOMETHING?

WRITE ABOUT IT.

When you have decided what to write about, it's time to begin.

To write a good nonfiction story you need:

Curiosity about something
Information sources
Facts
An outline
Conclusion

In a factual story, the information must be true.

COLLECT FACTS

ORGANIZE

OUTLINE

SUMMARIZE

LIMIT THE SUBJECT

You can't tell everything.
Choose carefully.

USE NOTES

Write important facts
down on note cards.

PREPARE AN OUTLINE

TITLE

A. BEGINNING
   a. Lead / hook

B. IMPORTANT FACTS
   a. Who
   b. What
   c. When
   d. Where
   e. How

C. SUMMARY

   a. Why

THE SAILOR'S WAY OF WRITING A GOOD NONFICTION STORY

Think of these questions before you sail on.

Beginning: What kind of nonfiction story are you writing?
What is your plan for writing the story? Do you have an outline?
Do you hook your reader with the first sentence?

Middle: Have you done your research?
Do you have good facts and information?
Do the facts lead your reader from one idea to another? Do you show both sides of the story?

End: What is your conclusion? Do your facts support it?
Can you summarize it in two or three sentences?
Does your conclusion make the reader think?

A poorly written nonfiction story confuses the reader by having too many facts. It's like trying to read too many maps at one time. It slows the reader to a stop.

A good nonfiction story has a clear focus and just enough facts to make the story interesting. It moves the reader along from beginning to end.

TEN RULES FOR A GOOD NONFICTION STORY

1. Choose your topic carefully.
2. Think of a catchy title.
3. Research your facts completely.
4. Prepare an outline.
5. Make note cards.
6. Use a strong hook or good lead sentence.
7. Write in clear, simple language.
8. Each paragraph must explain an idea.
9. Know when to end your story. Don't try to tell your reader everything.
10. Summarize your facts and have a strong ending.

STEP TWO

EDITING

Now that your story is written . . .

It's time to change hats.
You are now the editor.

What does an editor do?

An editor reads through the story carefully
and looks for these things:

1. Does the story make sense?
2. Does each sentence begin with a capital letter?
3. Do proper nouns begin with a capital letter?
4. Does each sentence end with the correct punctuation?
5. Are quotation marks used when there is conversation?
6. Is everything spelled correctly?
7. Is the story divided into paragraphs?
8. Are there any run-on sentences?

BE SURE TO READ YOUR STORY TO SOMEBODY ELSE TO SEE HOW THEY LIKE IT.

USE THESE PROOFREADING MARKS ON YOUR STORY.

Here are some proofreading marks that editors use. After you have marked your story, go back and fix it.

≡	Capital letter
⧸	Lowercase—use a small letter
¶	Begin a new paragraph here
sp	Spell out
ww	Wrong word—choose a better one
ℓ	Delete—take out where marked
#	Space needed here
∧	Something left out—put it in here

ILLUSTRATING

After you have written
and edited the story,
you're ready to . . .

Change hats again and
become the illustrator.

Where to begin?

Read your story again. But this time imagine pictures that will go with your words. Mark the exciting points because they are where your pictures could be. Decide how many pages and how many pictures you want your book to have.

Think about the mood or feeling of the story. Is it funny? Sad? Serious? Spooky? Match your pictures to the mood. Practice drawing your characters on scrap paper. Draw them different ways to see how they look.

You could use cartoon drawings if the story is funny. You could use dark colors if the story is spooky or sad. But if your story is about how a real caterpillar becomes a butterfly, you may want your pictures to be drawn true to life.

GRANDMOTHER

SERIOUS

GRANDMA

HAPPY

GRANNY

FUNNY

WHAT AGE LEVEL ARE YOU WRITING FOR?

It was my birthday. I had a cake.

At my birthday party everyone had a balloon.

If your story is for a very young child, use short sentences and bright colors.

If your story is for an older person, you can put more details into the style of your drawings.

STORYBOARD

A STORYBOARD SHOWS ALL THE PICTURES OF YOUR BOOK ON ONE PIECE OF PAPER.

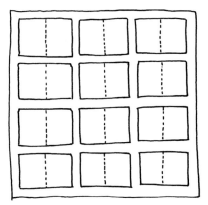

Before you begin the illustrations, make a plan.

Use a storyboard.

Draw or sketch in each square what your picture will look like. There's not enough room to draw the whole picture. You'll do that later. The storyboard is just a plan of how you will illustrate your book.

You can divide up your story in many different ways on your pages. This is called a layout.

A layout shows how you will organize the design of your book:

Where you will put the words

Where you will put the pictures

How many pages you will use

SAMPLE STORYBOARD

THE PARTS OF A BOOK

A BOOK CONSISTS OF A COVER, A TITLE PAGE, AND THE PAGES OF TEXT AND PICTURES. SOMETIMES BOOKS HAVE ENDPAPERS AND A DEDICATION PAGE.

THE TITLE PAGE:

A title page is the first page of your book. It has the title of the story, the name of the author, the name of the illustrator, and the date.

Print the title of your story and the author's name on this page. Who is the author? That's you!

It is nice to add the date that you wrote the book. You can design a border for decoration, draw something from your story as a "spot" illustration, or do both.

SAMPLE TITLE PAGES

THE DEDICATION PAGE:

A DEDICATION CAN BE WRITTEN ON THE BACK OF YOUR TITLE PAGE. IF YOU WROTE YOUR STORY FOR YOUR MOTHER, YOU CAN WRITE "FOR MOM."

THE INSIDE PAGES:

Most picture books that you buy in a store are 32 pages long and have less than 1,500 words. But your book can have as many pages as you want. You are drawing the pictures by hand.

You will have to decide where you want the pictures to go on each page. Where should the words go? How many sentences should be on each page? Use your storyboard to lay out the pages.

BE SURE TO KEEP YOUR WORDS ON ONE PAGE OR THE OTHER. YOU CAN PUT THE WORDS ON BOTH PAGES - BUT DON'T RUN THEM ACROSS THE CENTER FOLD. PICTURES CAN GO ACROSS THE CENTER FOLD IF YOU WISH, BUT NOT THE WORDS.

Center fold

PLANNING YOUR PICTURES

When you open a picture book, you see two pages at one time. Plan these pages to go together.

Sometimes the picture will go right across the two open pages. This is called a "two-page spread."

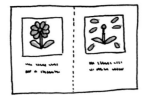

If you want to put different words and actions on each page, then you should separate them.

This can be done by using borders or smaller pictures.

You can also divide the spread so that the words are on one page and the picture is on the other page.

To make the pages match, use the same border on every page.

 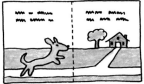 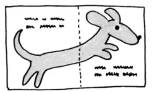 

Scene 1 CAMERA ACTION

There are different ways to present the same picture and words.

Pretend that you are looking through a camera and decide what to focus on. Like a movie director, you can vary the focus.

Sometimes draw the picture from very close up. Sometimes draw it from far away, to get in a whole scene or setting.

BE SURE THAT WHATEVER "STYLE" YOU CHOOSE, YOU ARE CONSISTENT THROUGHOUT THE BOOK. THAT MEANS THAT IN EVERY PICTURE, ON EVERY PAGE, YOU WILL DRAW IN THE SAME WAY. VARY THE "FOCUS" BUT KEEP THE STYLE THE SAME.

ILLUSTRATING YOUR PAGES

MATERIALS YOU WILL NEED:

- LEGAL-SIZED TYPING PAPER
- PENCIL
- ERASER
- BLACK FELT-TIP PEN
  OR
  BLACK THIN-TIP MARKER

Are you ready to draw?

1. Do you have a story?
2. Do you know what your characters look like?
3. Do you have your materials?
4. Do you have the story drawn on your storyboard?

If the answer is YES, then you are ready to draw.

 Carefully fold the sheets of paper in half, making the corners match. Make a nice sharp crease and then open the sheets up.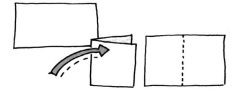

 With a pencil, number your pages on the bottom outside corners. Number one side only.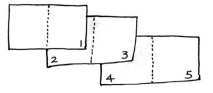

Be sure that page number one starts on the right-hand side.

Using your storyboard as a guide, lightly pencil in the drawings and words on each page. Ink your drawings. Erase the pencil. Hand print your words, or paste on typewritten ones.

Use the folded crease as your guide. It will be the centerfold of your book.

STORYBOARD

Dedicated to my science teacher, Mr. Meanbog

THE CASE OF THE DISAPPEARING SCIENCE PROJECT by JESS KIDDEN 1994

IT WAS RAINING. THERE WAS LIGHTNING AND THUNDER.

IT WAS TIME TO GO TO SCHOOL. I HAD TO BRING MY SCIENCE PROJECT THAT DAY.

Be sure to sketch in pencil first, then ink-in your drawings.

ADD COLOR TO YOUR PAGES

You can leave your drawings in black and white or you can add color.

If you want to make more than one copy of your book, this is the time to make photocopies of all your pages—before you color them. Then you can color the copies.

USE FELT MARKERS, CRAYONS, PENS, OR COLORED PENCILS TO COLOR. PAINT WOULD MAKE YOUR PAGES WRINKLY.

STEP FOUR

BINDING

After the story is written, edited, and illustrated, you are ready to . . .

Put on your binder's hat.

Assemble your book.

ASSEMBLING THE BOOK

Now it is time to bind your book. This means putting the pages together with a cover and endpapers. Here is how to put your book together.

Be sure to use a flat work area. Put newspaper under your work to keep your work surface neat.

MATERIALS —

- YOUR DRAWINGS
- GLUE STICK
- SCISSORS
- RULER

1. Begin with page one. Stack your pages one right after another.

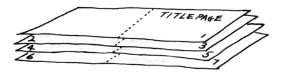

2. Fold each page. Pile the folded pages with page one on the bottom.

Be sure to fold the paper so that the drawing is inside and the blank side is out.

3. You have assembled all your pages, folded, in the right order. Turn the stack of pages so that the fold is in front of you.

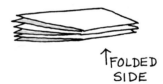

↑FOLDED
SIDE

4. Take the top sheet and flip it over toward you so that the fold is away from you.

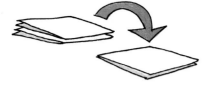

5. Use a glue stick on the back of your folded drawing. Make sure you come close to the edges, corners, and fold.

6. Take the next folded page. Line it up and set it on the glued side of the first page.

Be sure corners match, then smooth pages out.

7. Let the pages dry before you glue the next two pages together. Continue this until all your pages are glued. Be careful not to glue over the edge or your pages will stick together.

8. If you want endpapers, glue a plain (or colored) folded sheet to the front and back of your other pages.

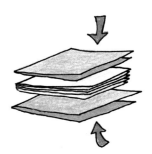

9. Fan out the pages. The blank sides are glued together and are connected at the folded sides. Set the book upright and fan out the pages so they can dry.

Be sure to check your pages. Make sure the corners and edges are even. If necessary, use scissors to trim the pages.

THE OUTSIDE COVER

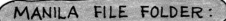

MANILA FILE FOLDER:

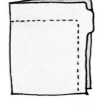

Using a ruler, measure the file folder to make a rectangle a little larger than your folded pages.

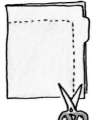

Cut out the rectangle through both sides of the folder.

MATERIALS —

MANILA FILE FOLDER
(white or colored)
OR POSTER BOARD

- GLUE STICK
- SCISSORS
- RULER
- PENCIL

OR POSTER BOARD

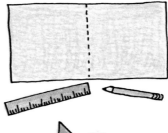

If you are using poster board, cut a rectangle a bit larger than your unfolded pages. Draw a straight line in the center of the poster board with a pencil.

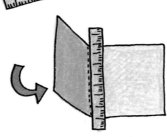

Using your ruler as a guide, fold the poster board on the line, making a sharp crease.

BINDER

1

COVER FOLDED

PAGES TOGETHER

2

OPEN COVER

GLUE BACK OF THE BACK PAGE

3

LINE UP BACK COVER AND BACK PAGE SO THAT THE CENTER FOLDS ARE MATCHED. PRESS DOWN AND SMOOTH FROM CENTER FOLD OUTWARD.

4

  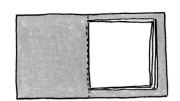

FOLD OVER SO THAT THE TITLE PAGE IS ON TOP AND THE FLAP IS DOWN.

5

APPLY GLUE ALONG THE EDGES OF FLAP

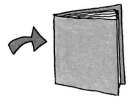

FOLD FRONT COVER OVER AND PRESS FLAT

6

OPEN UP FRONT COVER AND PRESS FLAP SMOOTH FROM CENTER FOLD OUTWARD

7

LET DRY

8

YOU CAN USE YOUR SCISSORS TO TRIM COVER DOWN TO A SMALL BORDER AROUND THE PAGES.

THE COVER DESIGN

Although the cover design is the first thing you see on a book, it is the last thing to draw.

Why? Because now you know your story very well. You know what's important in the story. You have drawn your characters many times on the pages and you have gotten very good at it.

Look through your pages. What drawing do you like best? Is your book an action story about a person, a thing, or an animal? If so, then show action on the cover.

What should be on the cover of a picture book?

1 The title of the book

2 The name of the author

3 A picture

4 The name of the illustrator

Be sure to design the cover so that people will want to read your book.

The title should show up in big letters or bright colors.

The picture can be above the words, below the words, between the words, or behind the words. The design can have a border on it or not. It is your design.

If your cover is white or a light color, you can draw your cover design right on it.

If your cover is dark, you can make your design on white paper, smaller than the cover. Then glue it on.

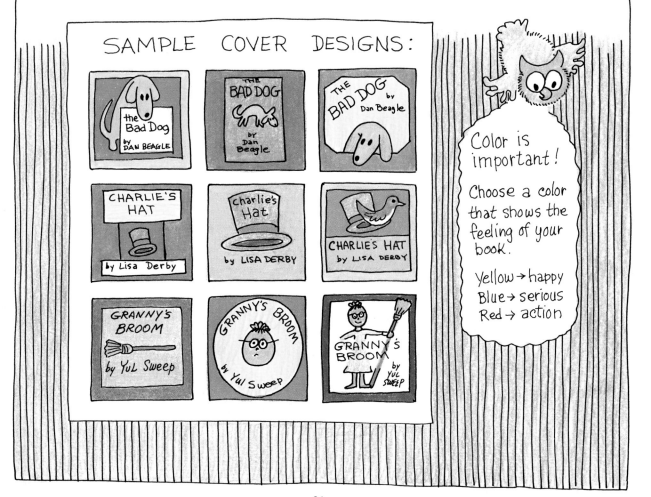

SAMPLE COVER DESIGNS:

the Bad Dog by DAN BEAGLE

THE BAD DOG by Dan Beagle

THE BAD DOG by Dan Beagle

CHARLIE'S HAT by Lisa Derby

Charlie's Hat by LISA DERBY

CHARLIE'S HAT by LISA DERBY

GRANNY'S BROOM by Yul Sweep

GRANNY'S BROOM by Yul Sweep

GRANNY'S BROOM by Yul Sweep

Color is important!

Choose a color that shows the feeling of your book.

Yellow → happy
Blue → serious
Red → action

You have written and edited your story,
drawn the illustrations,
and put it all together in a binding.

You've made a book!

PROMOTION

Now it's time to . . .

Put on your promotion hat and share your book with others.

You might ask your teacher or parents to throw an author's party. Invite your friends.

Send your grandparents or your favorite aunt an announcement about your book.

Take your book on an author's tour. Travel around your neighborhood and read it to your friends.

If you give a copy of your book away, be sure to sign your name on the title page. You may want to write a message, too.

ABOUT THE AUTHORS

Donna Guthrie is the author of half a dozen books for children, including *The Witch Who Lives Down the Hall* and *A Rose for Abby*. A former teacher who lives in Los Gatos, California, she has traveled widely to speak to children about her experiences as a writer.

A teacher and librarian as well as a writer, Nancy Bentley lives in Colorado Springs, Colorado. Her previous children's books include *I've Got Your Nose!* and the Busy Body Board Book series.

Katy Keck Arnsteen, also a Colorado Springs resident, has illustrated over twenty-five books, including five of her own and five by Donna Guthrie. She brings a background in fine arts and education to her picture books.